The Dao of Unrep
Chinese Experienc

Daniel York Loh

methuen | drama

LONDON · NEW YORK · OXFORD · NEW DELHI · SYDNEY

METHUEN DRAMA
Bloomsbury Publishing Plc
50 Bedford Square, London, WC1B 3DP, UK
1385 Broadway, New York, NY 10018, USA
29 Earlsfort Terrace, Dublin 2, Ireland

BLOOMSBURY, METHUEN DRAMA and the Methuen
Drama logo are trademarks of Bloomsbury Publishing Plc

First published in Great Britain 2024

A catalogue record for this book is available from the British Library.

Library of Congress Control Number: 2024938236.

ISBN: PB: 978-1-3505-0866-8
ePDF: 978-1-3505-0867-5
eBook: 978-1-3505-0868-2

Series: Modern Plays

Typeset by Mark Heslington Ltd, Scarborough, North Yorkshire
Printed and bound in Great Britain

To find out more about our authors and books visit
www.bloomsbury.com and sign up for our newsletters.

Kakilang presents:

The Dao of Unrepresentative British Chinese Experience (Butterfly Dream)

By Daniel York Loh

Cast

Melody Chikakane Brown

Aruhan Galieva

Daniel York Loh

Creative and Production Team

Erin Guan	*Video and Projection Designer*
QianEr Jin	*Set and Costume Designer*
Joe Price	*Lighting Designer*
Vivi Wei	*Stage Manager*
Florian Lim	*Assistant Stage Manager*
Pete Rickards for eStage	*Production Manager*
Ching-Lin (Irene) Peng	*Production Assistant*
Kendell Foster	*Video Technician*
Sanli Wang	*Lighting Assistant*
Si Rawlinson	*Movement Director*
Tobi Poster Su	*Material Performance Consultant*
Valerie Mo	*Assistant Director*
Natalie Chan	*Producer*
An-Ting 安婷	*Composer & Sound Designer*
Alice Kornitzer	*Director & Dramaturge*

Publicity by **Chloé Nelkin Consulting Public Relations**

For Kakilang

Joey Jepps General Manager

Katrina Man Arts & Community Producer

Sandy Wan Head of Marketing & Audience Development

Cover credit: Photography by **Jennifer Lim**, Design by **Émilie Chen**

The Dao of Unrepresentative British Chinese Experience (Butterfly Dream) is supported by:

Arts Council England
John Ellerman Foundation

Cockayne – Grants for the Arts: a donor advised fund held at The London Community Foundation.

Battersea Arts Centre

Kakilang and Daniel York Loh also wish to thank the following for their help with this production:

Maia Tamrakar, Battersea Arts Centre, Jennifer Lim, Caridad Svich, Donald Shek, Marie McCarthy, Ling Tan, Jessica Hung Han Yun, Scott Black, Amanda Maud, Becky Barry, Soho Theatre, Theatre Royal Stratford East, Independent Theatre Council, the members of BEATS: JM Arrow, Bec Boey, Julian Chou-Lambert, Rosa Fong, Matt Lim, Mingyu Lin, Chip Nguyen, Lucy Sheen, Paul Sng and Dr. Diana Yeh.

About Kakilang

Kakilang 自己人 produces and presents world-class interdisciplinary art from a wide spectrum of Southeast and East Asian voices. We pioneer work across multiple art forms and showcase artists working at the intersection of diverse practices.

Kakilang (formerly Chinese Arts Now) was founded in 2005 and became a National Portfolio Organisation supported by Arts Council England in 2018. Since then we have partnered with the Barbican, Southbank Centre, Rich Mix, Soho Theatre, The Place, Horizon, Leicester Curve, York Theatre Royal, Cambridge Junction, Oxford Contemporary Music, LSO St Luke's, BFI, Young Vic, Tamasha, Dance Umbrella, and more.

The company was rebranded as Kakilang in September 2022. The name Kakilang (自己人) meaning 'one of us' in the Hokkien dialect, evoking kinship and affinity, is widely used amongst East and Southeast Asian diasporic groups. For us, our Kakilang are people who come together through art, and who champion diverse voices and communities.

In 2022, Kakilang won Arts Council England's Digital Culture Award (Storytelling) for *every dollar is a soldier/with money you're a dragon* created by An-Ting 安婷 and Daniel York Loh, co-produced with Two Temple Place, as well as being nominated in the 2023 UK Theatre Awards (Digital Innovation category) for our production *HOME X*.

Our vibrant community of wonderful supporters serves as the backbone of our mission at Kakilang. It enables us to champion and elevate Southeast and East Asian voices in the global arts landscape. Each supporter plays an integral role in empowering us to push boundaries, celebrate diversity, and amplify the voices of emerging and established artists alike. Through their commitment, we are empowered to explore new artistic frontiers, cultivate groundbreaking interdisciplinary works, and challenge conventional norms, thereby reshaping and enriching the cultural landscape of our world.

Kakilang Supporters

Arts Council England

Bagri Foundation

Cockayne – Grants for the Arts: a donor advised fund held at The London Community Foundation

John Ellerman Foundation

Paul Hamlyn Foundation

To all our supporters, thank you.

SOHO THEATRE is London's most vibrant producer for new theatre, comedy and cabaret. Our central London venue is established as one of UK's busiest with a buzzing bar and lively audiences. Our roots date back to the early 1970s at the Soho Poly Theatre. Small but influential, Soho Poly was radical and relevant, capturing the excitement and innovation of its time. Today our work is wide-ranging, drawing from this fringe heritage, and adding a queer, punk, counter-culture flavour.

We champion voices that challenge from outside of the mainstream, and sometimes from within it too. We value entertainment and a great night out. We produce and co-produce new plays, work with associate artists and present the best new emerging theatre companies and comedians. We present the early work of countless UK artists (many who become industry giants), and we present many international artists' London debuts. As important as the work on our stages, we have a thriving variety of artist and talent development programmes, artists under commission and in development, and two new writing awards including the national Verity Bargate Award for new playwrights.

Work extends beyond our venues with a full touring programme and strong international connections with New York, Melbourne and Mumbai. Edinburgh Fringe is a huge part of our year, we present many shows and scout hundreds more and we are the UK's leading presenter of Indian comedians. Our filmed comedy specials can be seen on international airlines and Soho Theatre Player. And in 2025 our second London venue, Soho Theatre Walthamstow, opens. Soho Theatre is a charity and social enterprise.

Performer – Melody Chikakane Brown

Melody is of British/Japanese heritage and was born and raised in York. She trained at Manchester Poly. Theatre work includes: *Box of Delights*, *Measure for Measure* and *The Taming of the Shrew* (Royal Shakespeare Company); *Midsummer Mechanicals* (Shakespeare's Globe and Splendid); *The Good Person of Szechwan* (Sheffield Crucible, Lyric Hammersmith and English Touring Theatre); *Wind in the Wiltons* (Wilton's Music Hall); *Sour Cherry Soup* and *Two Pairs of Eyes* (Inroads); *Henry V* (Shakespeare at the Tobacco Factory); *House* and *Garden* and *Bubbles* (Watermill Theatre); *Tamburlaine* (New Earth | Arcola, tour); *Last Journey* (Pentabus); *History Boys* (Selladoor, tour); *Free Folk* (Forest Forge) and *Fungus the Bogeyman* (Pilot Theatre).

She recently appeared as Karen in BBC Limelight's radio drama, *Money Gone*, and as Ivy in Radio 4's *The Chatterleys*.

Melody plays bass and sings with British Asian Country Punk band Wondermare, and Hastings' garage rock legends, Thee Leatherettes.

Performer – Aruhan Galieva

Theatre includes: *Fair Maid of the West*, *Comedy of Errors* (RSC), *ECO MANIAC* (Writer/Performer, Omnibus Theatre), *Kinky Boots* (New Wolsey Theatre, Ipswich and Queen's Theatre), *Gin Craze* (Royal & Derngate and China Plate co-production in partnership with English Touring Theatre), *My Cousin Rachel* (Theatre Royal Bath), *Twelfth Night* (Southwark Playhouse), *Much Ado About Nothing*, *The Two Gentlemen of Verona*, *King John* (Shakespeare's Globe), *Romeo and Juliet*, *Twelfth Night* (Watermill Theatre), *Bakkhai* (Almeida Theatre).

Television includes: *The Emily Atack Show*, *Doctor Who*, *Black Mirror*, *Doctors*, *Glasgow Girls*, *Whitechapel*.

Film and Short Film includes: *Anna Karenina* (Working Title), *A Quiet Life* (BBC), *Aquarium* (BFI), *Coalition Fangirls* (BFI/Roundhouse), *COMEDY SHOTS* (C4).

Radio includes: *Time of the Week*, *The Passport* and *This Week Is Family Week* (BBC)

Aruhan received an Off-West End (Offie) Nomination for her critically acclaimed portrayal of Lauren in the UK Revival of *Kinky Boots*. As a comedian she won the 2022 Luke Rollason Memorial Bursary Award for Emerging Alternative Comedians.

As a singer she has performed as Vocal Soloist at venues such as the Royal Albert Hall, Carnegie Hall (NY), Tokyo City Opera Hall, and has headlined at the Royal Festival Hall and Midem Festival (Cannes).

Writer and Performer – Daniel York Loh

Stage plays include *The Fu Manchu Complex* (Ovalhouse/Moongate) and *Forgotten* 遗忘. (Arcola/Plymouth Theatre Royal/Moongate/New Earth), as well as for the Royal Court's *Living Newspaper* and *Living Archive, Silent Disco in the Sky* (Northern Stage 'Scroll' collection), *No Time For Tears* with Ghost & John for Moongate's *We R Not Virus* online collection.

He is one of twenty-one 'writers of colour' featured in the best-selling essay collection *The Good Immigrant*. He is Associate Artistic Director of Kakilang with whom he co-created and performed in *every dollar is a soldier/with money you're a dragon* which won the 2022 Arts Council Digital Culture Award (Storytelling). For Papergang: *Invisible Harmony*无形的和谐 (Southbank Centre/2020 CAN Festival) and *Freedom Hi* 自由閪 (VAULT Festival)

As an actor he has performed at the Royal Shakespeare Company, National Theatre, Donmar Warehouse, Royal Court, Hampstead Theatre, Finborough, Theatre503, Gate, Bristol Old Vic, Edinburgh Traverse and most recently in *Dr. Semmelweis* in the West End, as well as extensively in Singapore and in the feature films *Rogue Trader*, *The Beach*, *The Receptionist* and *Scarborough*. He is currently (during production dates) appearing in *Sam Wu is NOT Afraid of Ghosts* at Polka Theatre.

Director – Alice Kornitzer

Alice Kornitzer's work spans new writing, adaptations, classics and documentary across stage, screen, TV and digital formats – as director, dramaturge, creative and cultural producer.

Alice trained at Queen Margaret University, Edinburgh, and the University of Bristol and has worked across Europe, UK and in the US.

Their production of *Chummy* at the White Bear Theatre, London, by BAFTA-winning John Foster garnered four Offie-nominations including Best Director. They are a recipient of the European Theatre Conference Artist Residency. Alice is the founder and artistic director of Sharp Image Company, producing international new work, and Pick

Up Productions – a touring company for artists from alternative access pathways performing the classics with a twist on a pickup truck. Next to theatre, they executive produce digital, streaming and video productions for TV and film formats and are a published writer.

Being an interdisciplinary artist, they use mixed media and formats to create work challenging cultural, political and social narratives.

Producer – Natalie Chan

Natalie is a tenacious, innovative arts leader and independent producer based in Hong Kong and UK. She is currently Executive Director at Streatham Space Project.

Credits includes as Associate Producer for *Best of Enemies* in the West End; Producer for *This Is Not A Show About Hong Kong*, which won Fringe First and New Diorama Theatre and Underbelly's Untapped Award in 2022; Consultant for *WILD the Musical* (City Chamber Orchestra of Hong Kong).

As a committed change-maker to support fellow Global Majority arts leaders, she was an innovator and Agent for Change with Artistic Directors of the Future.

Composer and Sound Designer An-Ting 安婷

An-Ting 安婷 is a versatile artist who thrives in piano, electronic compositions, and various other forms of artistic expression. Drawing from her life experiences, she weaves diverse encounters into her creations, merging music with other art forms to delve into the depths of the human experience.

Between 2018 and 2023, she led the National Portfolio Organisation Kakilang, placing emphasis on establishing an artist-led structure, generating new narratives by Southeast and East Asian heritage artists, and encouraging cross-artform collaborations. Original work created for Kakilang includes *Bats and Beats* (Southbank's Soundstate Festival/Shanghai), the *Augmented Chinatown 2.0* app created with Joel Tan and Donald Shek, the award-winning *every dollar is a soldier/with money you're a dragon* with Daniel York Loh, Si Rawlinson, Ian Gallagher, Christine Ting-Urquhart, Cheng Yu, Wang Xiao and Chloe Wing, and *HOME X,* a gaming/VR/dance mixed-media piece created with Ian Gallagher and Donald Shek (Barbican Pit, nominated for UK Theatre Award-Digital Innovation)

Her background is grounded in a unique fusion of science and art, holding a degree in Chemistry from National Taiwan University, alongside a MMus and PhD in performance from the Royal Academy of Music.

Set and Costume Designer – QianEr Jin

QianEr is a London-based set and costume designer, specializing in story driven, site-specific experiences and design-led devised pieces. She thrives on collaborative ventures and embraces the fusion of media and new technology.

She is a RCSSD alumni and her recent credits include: *Tribe* (Young Vic) and *Modest* (Middle Child, national tour)

Website: www.qianerjin.com

Video and Projection Designer – Erin Guan

Erin Guan is a London-based scenographer and interactive installation artist from China. Her work spans across intercultural performances and minority voices. Her recent theatre projects include *The Dao of Unrepresentative British Chinese Experience* (Kakilang x Soho Theatre), *Romeo and Juliet* (Polka Theatre), *Turandot* (The Opera Makers & Ellandar x Arcola Theatre), *Pied Piper* (Battersea Arts Centre), *The Apology* (New Earth Theatre x Arcola Theatre), *A Gig for Ghosts* (Forty Five North x Soho Theatre Upstairs), *Pressure Drop* (Immediate Theatre), *Unchain Me* (Dreamthinkspeak x Brighton Festival), *Prayers for a Hungry Ghost* (Barbican Open Lab), *Foxes* (Defibrillator Theatre x Theatre503), *Tokyo Rose* (Burnt Lemon Theatre) and both immersive game theatre *Talk* and *The House Never Wins* (Kill The Cat Theatre). Her recent TV work includes costume design for *East Mode* S2 with Nigel Ng (Comedy Central x Channel 5).

Lighting Designer – Joe Price

Joe studied at the Royal Welsh College of Music & Drama and is now based in Bristol. He received the 2015 Francis Reid Award for Lighting Design and his work on *A Woman Walks Into A Bank* at Theatre503 was nominated for the 2023 Offie Award for Lighting Design.

Credits include: *My Name Is Rachel Corrie* (Young Vic); *Outlier* (Bristol Old Vic); *Petula* (National Theatre Wales); *The World's Wife* (Welsh

National Opera); *Redefining Juliet* (Barbican); *Wendy, Five Children and It, Rapunzel* (The Egg); *Revealed* (Tobacco Factory); *Heads Will Roll* (Told by an Idiot); *Heather* (Bush Theatre); *Quality Street* (Northern Broadsides); *Bitcoin Boi* (Riverfront Newport); *The Turn of the Screw* (RWCMD); *Ask Me Anything, Goldfish Bowl* (Paper Birds); *Kite* (UK and China tour); *Conditionally* (Soho Theatre); *Mrs Dalloway, Carmen, How to Date a Feminist* (Arcola Theatre); *Fossils* (Brits Off Broadway NYC); *Dinosaurs and All That Rubbish* (Roustabout); *What Songs May Do* (Dance City); *Box Clever, Killymuck, Breathe* (Bunker Theatre); *Merboy* (Omnibus Theatre); *Peter Pan* (Barn Theatre); *Frankie Vah, The Remains of Logan Dankworth* (Luke Wright); *Let the Right One In* (Arts Ed); *Magnificence, A Third* (Finborough Theatre); *Some Girl(s)* (Park Theatre); *Around the World in 80 Days* (Theatre Royal Winchester); *Y Twr* (Invertigo).

Lighting Assistant – Sanli Wang

Sanli Wang is an interdisciplinary artist, theatermaker and researcher based in London. She recently graduated from the College of Central Saint Martins at UAL and meanwhile trained at the National Theatre.

She has contributed to performances as a lighting designer, dramaturg and director.

She focuses on understanding and interpreting the world through theatrical expression, drawing from sociological and philosophical perspectives. She is deeply committed to integrating personal experiences as a theatre practitioner and audience member as well as reflections on creations into her work within the performances.

In her academic pursuits, she explores directorial authorship and theatre ontology under the content of multidisciplinary collaborations.

As a theatermaker, she has worked at Zaha Hadid Architects Gallery, New Diorama Theatre, Camden People Theatre and Platform Theatre. She was engaged in site-specific projects presented in Greenwich Market and Blackburn funded by the Arts Council.

Movement Director – Si Rawlinson

Si Rawlinson is a British Chinese choreographer, born in Hong Kong with English and Chinese heritage. A theatremaker with a background in dance, his practice is interdisciplinary, mixing hip hop and contemporary dance, physical performance, and theatre. His work has been performed at leading venues in the UK including The Place, Sadler's Wells, Southbank Centre, Birmingham Hippodrome, Curve Theatre, and Nottingham Playhouse. He has also worked with acclaimed artists including Gary Clarke, Alesandra Seutin, Requardt & Rosenberg, and has also danced in commercials and on film (Marvel/Disney). Other credits include the role of Kazego/Puppeteer in the Royal Shakespeare Company's Olivier-Award-winning stage adaptation of *My Neighbour Totoro* at the Barbican.

Material Performance Consultant – Tobi Poster-Su

Tobi Poster-Su is a UK-based theatremaker and scholar who specialises in puppetry and devised, cross disciplinary work. As co-artistic director of Wattle and Daub, Tobi has co-created and performed in *Chang and Eng and Me (and Me)* (Kakilang Festival), *The Depraved Appetite of Tarrare the Freak* (Wilton's Music Hall) and *Triptych* (Mayfest). They have worked as a puppetry director and puppeteer on shows including Tom Morris's *A Christmas Carol* (Bristol Old Vic) and *Heidi: A Goat's Tale* (the egg) and RSC and Improbable's *My Neighbour Totoro* (the Barbican). Tobi leads the MA in Puppetry at Wimbledon College of Arts and is completing an AHRC-funded PhD (*Towards a Critical Puppetry: Racialisation and Material Performance in the Twenty-First Century*) at Queen Mary University of London. He is co-convener of the TaPRA Bodies and Performance working group.

Assistant Director – Valerie Mo

Valerie Mo (she/her) is a Chinese queer theatremaker based in London and Shanghai. Her passion lies in crafting narratives that explore the intricacies of womanhood, intimate relationships, and cultural identities through bold and imaginative expressions. She has recently featured in Act II Springboard Festival 2024 as one of the fifteen selected young directors. Recent works include *things to say when I see you in person* (Arts Centre Hounslow) and *Metamorphoses* (The Cockpit).

Production Manager – Pete Rickards for eStage

Pete is Director of Production with production management company eStage. His career has seen him undertake numerous production management roles, tour management, as well as technical and design roles across multiple disciplines. He has managed productions and touring artists worldwide at venues and festivals such as the Barbican, the Roundhouse, Hackney Empire, Busan International Performing Arts Festival, Merlin Attractions, Birmingham Repertory Theatre, Bristol Old Vic, Schaubühne Berlin, Soho Theatre, Liverpool Everyman, Battersea Arts Centre, Midlands Arts Centre, Birmingham NEC, Wacken Open Air, Nottingham Playhouse and multiple UK/EU/Asian tours. A musician and artist in his own right with a backlog of hectic onstage stories, he enjoys working with likeminded people and gig theatre mixes all aspects of his passions, making working on 'Dao' a 'real joy'.

Stage Manager – Vivi Wei

Vivi Wei is a stage manager, performer and educator from China. Her passion lies in exploring the impact of technology on performance art through multi-disciplinary approaches, particularly in migrant theatre.

Her work spans the UK and China, her recent stage management work includes The *Dao of Unrepresentative British Chinese Experience* (Kakilang, Soho Theatre), *Cinderella* (Brixton House), *Project Atom Boi* (Camden People's Theatre, Artist Choice Award in VAULT Festival), *USELESS* (Brixton House), *Lessons on Revolution* (Carmen Collective Undone Theatre), *Saving Face* (Curve Theatre, The Place) and *Dreamaker Theatre Festival* (Changjiang Theatre, Shanghai).

She is also a keen educator and performer, on her way to exploring innovative approaches to working with young people, as well as acting on stage; credits include *Assembly Week* (Company Three), *KATZENMUSIK* (London Youth Theatre), *Hansel and Gretel* (Dreamaker Productions, Shanghai), *Someone* (Pearl Theatre, Shanghai), *Christmas Carol* (Pearl Theatre, Shanghai) and *Woo Woolf* (Camden People's Theatre).

Vivi Wei is also the co-founder of award-winning multidisciplinary theatre company Ensemble_Not_Found.

Assistant Stage Manager – Florian Lim

Florian Lim is a Singaporean Chinese theatremaker, stage manager and producer. They are the founder of investigative theatre company Burning Attic, leading the creation of a play on trans healthcare, *Patient is a Verb* (Camden People's Theatre). Recent stage management credits include *Silence* (Queens Hornchurch, Leicester

Curve, Birmingham Rep, HOME MCR), *First Trimester* (Battersea Arts Centre), *Marty and the Party* (Northern Stage, HOME MCR, Southbank Centre). They were a 2022 Optimists Producer with China Plate Theatre, and as a producer they support new work by interdisciplinary artists, such as *The Afters* by Shane ShayShay Konno (Pleasance) and *FUTURA GLITCH* by Livia Rita (Sadler's Wells). Part of the Bitten Peach, they sometimes perform drag, burlesque and poetry as fox devil-deity Gen de Fauxx.

The Dao of Unrepresentative British Chinese Experience (Butterfly Dream)

Dedicated to the memory of Patrick York (Loh)

/ indicates overlapping dialogue

To be performed by any number of performers of any gender of any ability or disability of any Central, Southeast or East Asian heritage

The Sage 先哲上部

At first, we thought we'd refer to him as 'The Sage'. Didn't we?

Yeah, because it's easier to say for most of us and if it's easier to say it's easier to remember and the story's easier to follow and, here in the West, complicated Chinese names are too hard to say and even harder to remember and render the story incomprehensible

But then we thought

Fuck that

And we asked

What is 'Story'?

Does it mean there's a beginning, middle and end?

And if there's none of those things does it need to be 'followed'?

Can we experience it like a dream?

The Dao –

(I know, bear with us, we'll get there)

The Dao of our story means there is no linear structure. We fly on the photon of parallel duality. We take flights of fancy

So that means we can weigh in on an unfamiliar Chinese name

Zhuangzi

Zhuang . . . zi

Perhaps we can all practise

Zhuang . . . zi

Or Zhuang Zhou (I know I know it's complicated)

Zhaungzi was a philosopher born in the kingdom of Song in
what we now call 'China' but what was then a bunch of
kingdoms or states which occupied a geographical space
where they fought wars against each other and attempted
very hard to be the one to 'unify' all the rest from the
'Middle' – the 'Middle' being wherever they were

There's only one thing we really know about the life of
Zhuangzi and it's this –

One time King Wei of Chu wanted to make Zhuangzi a chief
minister

But Zhuangzi just laughed

And said –

'A thousand measures of silver. That's a tidy wad. And to be a
high noble. That's schmancy. But have you not seen the
victim-ox for the border sacrifice? The clue is in the name.
The victim-ox gets lavishly but carefully fed for several years,
and draped in bling with rich embroidery so the victim-ox is
gaudy enough to enter the Grand Temple . . . where the
victim-ox is slaughtered. When the time comes the victim-ox
might wish he was just an orphan-piglet. But it's too late!
Now fuck off and do not vex me with your presence. I'd
rather chill in a filthy ditch than be subject to rules and
restrictions in the court of some despot. I prefer to live my
best life with my own free will'

Honestly

If he'd never ever written anything after that I think his
place as a great master would be assured on that story alone

Maybe we should stop calling Zhuangzi 'him'. Zhuangzi was
big on opposites being the same – success / failure, fame /
infamy, happy / sad – I'm pretty sure Zhuangzi would be
non-binary

Zhuangzi once dreamed Zhuangzi was a butterfly

Fluttering about in perfect happiness like a butterfly would

The butterfly followed their whims where their whims took them and the butterfly knew nothing of Zhuangzi

Suddenly Zhuangzi awoke and there Zhuangzi was

Zhuangzi in the flesh

But Zhuangzi couldn't figure out if Zhuangzi had been dreaming Zhuangzi was a butterfly or if Zhuangzi was a butterfly dreaming they were Zhuangzi

Sometimes

I dream I'm Chinese

Where The Twain Meets 两方相遇的地方

The Twain did meet and the Twain did mix in the blood
     inside my veins
Where East meets West for dumpling soup and they
     complain about the rain
They read the *Global Times* and watch GB News and
     exchange which flag to wave
They imperialise then decolonise and start all over again

The NSL and the Borders Bill swim together inside my blood
They want to lock me up and send me back, close the door
     with an angry thud
Then make me cook their lunch and dress me up and
     mispronounce my name
East and West busting up my spleen fighting hard to stake
     their claim

They talk of battleships in the Taiwan Straits and their love
     of boba tea
Taking back control with the People's Will which says we
     vote to Leave
My vital organs are a bloody mess with this much trouble
     and strife
'cuz West and East can't synchronise on their choice for my
     way of life

They're going mahjong with a bad sixteen in this battle for
     my soul
East and West think they're both best-placed to turn my half
     into a whole
God saves the Queen on arteriole highways where they
     march with the volunteers
And East and West bypass my heart with a pair of garden
     shears

No matter what the language I attempt East and West both
     take the piss
My lack of culture cred is the Twain they meet in a state of
     permanent bliss

It reassures them, haute-coutures them, that I'll just never
    make the grade
Like an understudy who didn't learn the lines and is grateful
    to be cooled in their shade

East and West fight to the death now tearing my being in
    half
Like a two-headed snake or psychotic hydra whose rage is
    off the graph
Though the Twain did meet, fox eyes can't see and they just
    can't co-exist
East and West in my large intestine with each other get all
    nativist

In this culture war I couldn't choose a side, I just didn't have
    a team
'They're tearing me apart' I wail and whine like a hapa-mix
    Jimmy Dean
I carry West and East inside my bowel where I long for their
    sweet release
Cuz that Twain is bust and needs be fixed by those two sides
    I just can't please

'And now all you sisters & brothers (and siblings who are
transitioning between) of East & Southeast Asian persuasion
(that's **ESEA** for short) who wanna see some increased
pervasion of mainstream equation and an actual invasion of
our media representation . . .

. . . here at Team **ESEA** Podcast where we bond over food
and boba and movies and all things **ESEA** and what it means
to be **ESEA** and uplift our fellow **ESEAs** and spread that
#ESEALOVE . . .

Here at Team ESEA Podcast today we are hosting for your
delectation affirmation and identification . . .

An all-important Community Conversation on Racial Slurs
Directed Towards **ESEA** People . . .'

Playground Politics 游乐场政治

'Chinese

'Japanese

'Dirty knees

'What are these?'

I have a dream where I'm racially abused in the playground

'Chinese

'Japanese

'Dirty knees

'What are these?'

Or am I racially abused in the playground dreaming that I'm dreaming I was never actually racially abused in the playground but dreaming of being racially abused in the playground from the comfort of a white middle-class theatre setting?

Is that gaslighting?

'Chinese

'Japanese

'Dirty knees

'What are these?'

I was five years old when it happened

– Hello

– Hello

– Are you Chinese?

– Yeah

– HAAAAAAAAAAA!!!!

'*Chinese*

'*Japanese*

'*Dirty knees*

'*What are these?*'

It was really that basic

And it went on and on again and again

– Hello

– Hello

– Are you Chinese?

– Yeah

– HAAAAAAAAAAA!!!!

'*Chinese*

'*Japanese*

'*Dirty knees*

'*What are these?*'

I didn't even know what it meant

– **Hi Team ESEA Podcast, just wanna say, I #ESEALove the podcast and I also wanna say that . . .**

I just knew it wasn't kind

– **. . . I mean often it felt like the young person reciting the lines would move the corners of their eyes up on the word Chinese and down on Japanese, before touching their knees and then grabbing or even exposing their own breasts . . .**

What the f –

- **Yeah yeah yeah, the performer's fingers make upward-slanting eyes for Chinese and downward-slanting eyes for Japanese . . .**

I see . . .

- *See I really don't like it because it associates Asians with either poor hygiene or subservience. Dirty knees could indicate a need to wash, but they also suggest that the person kneels a lot . . .*

Oh!

- *. . . exposing one's breasts in the 'look at these' line also alludes to promiscuity*

I'm seven years old I don't know about these things

- Hello

- Hello

- Are you Chinese?

- Yeah

- HAAAAAAAAAAA!!!!

'*Chinese*

'*Japanese*

'*Dirty knees*

'*What are these?*'

- **Yeah but, come on, guys, kids have a lot of stupid rhymes for jump rope and clapping games in the playground. At least we did, I would guess kids still do. I never thought it was a put down to anyone, you know? Just fun**

'Fun'

- **Thank you, Team ESEA Podcast, for letting me partake in the conversation as . . . an ally. I'd just like to posit**

that this rhyme is cultural. It points out the meaning of a Japanese word for breasts. The Japanese word is pronounced 'knee knee', as in two knees, and some may think *** are dirty. This explains the breast gestures. An example of this mispronunciation today can be found in the mispronunciation of the state bird of Hawaii (the Nene Goose), often mispronounced 'knee knee', which could offend Japanese people or make them laugh at you

That's . . . complicated

– *The upsetting thing was that other kids that normally did not behave this way would then join in . . .*

That's true! It's so catchy, it's actually . . . compelling . . .

'*Chinese*

'*Japanese*

'*Dirty knees*

'*What are these?*'

'In my opinion I thought it was a way to try to offer a sense of gratitude, appreciation and acknowledgement for two cultures that are often overlooked and underappreciated. . . . Chinese, eyes up, over-looked. Japanese, eyes down, under-appreciated. Dirty knees, hard-working people often have to get a bit dirty. Look at these, notice these or . . . them'

That's . . . a reach

– **I only ever saw boys do it, not girls**

'*Chinese*

'*Japanese*

'*Dirty knees*

'*What are these?*'

No, there's some girls joining in as well. It's so catchy

– **See, I think that 'Dirty knees' comes from the fact that foreigners living in Asia had Chinese domestic staff who would, of course, spend time on their knees cleaning floors. 'Look at these' would refer to the difference in the size of Western and Asian breasts, which is often a source of wonder to Asians unused to seeing Western women**

Oh so it's a question or enquiry like –

'Chinese

'Japanese

'Dirty knees

'What are these？？？'

– **When I was a kid I never took it as racist, just . . . we got different-shaped eyes innit. Didn't mean we were inferior**

And the bit about the knees? /

> – *It was just a funny rhyme! Too many woke idiots call it racism*

– that's just so it rhymes?

> – **I don't think it was ever meant to make fun of anyone . . . I knew a girl who used to say it and then flash boys by lifting her skirt. She also used to tell us to kiss her c/*****

– Hello

– Hello

– Are you Chinese?

– Yeah

– HAAAAAAAAAAA!!!!

'Chinese

'Japanese

'Dirty knees

'What are these?'

On and on

- Hello

- Hello

- Are you Chinese?

- Yeah

- HAAAAAAAAAAA!!!!

'Chinese

'Japanese

'Dirty knees

'What are these?'

I often wonder why I didn't –

- Hello

- Hello

- Are you Chinese?

- No

- . . .

- . . .

- . . .

- Oh. Right

'Me Chinese, me play joke, me put peepee in your Coke . . .'

I was the only Chinese kid at that school. I was the only Chinese kid I'd ever even seen. And I wasn't even really Chinese

–   Do you live in a take-away?

–   No, my dad works for British Rail

–   . . .

–   Oh

One day the teacher was giving us a lesson on race and nationality

In the 1970s

–   **. . . generally, it's the rule that you take the nationality of where you were born and the race of your father**

–   Miss

–   **Yes, Tommy**

–   That means this one here's not English

–   **Well . . . they are . . . they're just –**

–   Nah, but you said –

–   **What I meant / was –**

–   You said you take the race of your dad and this one's dad's from China / –

Actually he's not from / China

–   **I know what I said Tommy, but they were born here so they're / English**

–   But their dad's a chi / nk –

–   **That's not the point / Tommy**

–   So they're a chi / nk –

–   **They're English / Tommy –**

- They can't be English if their dad's a chink / Miss
- **Don't be pedantic, please / Tommy**
- They're not English, they're not one of us, they're a chink
- **Oh shut the fuck up, Tommy, you rancerous little shit!**

'Chinese

'Japanese

'Dirty knees

'What are these?'

'Fucking chink!'

'Ching Chong Chinaman!'

'Harroooo'

It all got too much

So I trashed the classroom

(DOES SO)

- **Violent tendencies**
- **Reads too many comics**
- **I spoke to the father**
- **How was that?**
- **His accent . . . I don't think his English is very good**

My father doesn't know any other language apart from English, sir

- **The parents do their best but . . . it's obviously difficult**
- **Clear behavioural problems, anti-social disorder /**
- **The trouble is they come to this country without learning about our sense of humour**

- **No, well /**

- **Nor sense of fair play and good manners**

- **No well /**

- **I mean, we never actually colonised *them* did we /**

- **I can prescribe this medication**

- **Oh! Lovely!**

- **That should calm them down a bit. Make them less . . .
  aggressive**

Oh cool, sir. Are these pills gonna make me immune to
people calling me a 'chink' all day?

Or will they make me feel not so alone?

Or will they even let me dream of being a butterfly?

- Hello

- Hello

- You're Chinese

- Kind of

- So am I

- Teacher said

- I'm from Hong Kong

- I don't know where that is

- My name's Siu Fai

- Hello

- My English isn't very good

- Your English is fine

- I sound strange

- Your accent's a bit different that's all, the other kids will take the piss out of it

- Do you eat Chinese food?

- Only when we go to my grandma's house

- I eat Chinese food every day

- My mum's English

- Do you play football

- I play right-back in the school team

- Will they let me play in the school team?

- Mr Nolan says I'm a big lad for a chink so I need to get stuck in more

- I'm really quick, I play up front

- I wanna play up front

- What else do you wanna be?

- I wanna be a butterfly. Then I might not get called names anymore. And if I did I could just fly away

'Chinese

Japanese

'Dirty knees

'What are these?'

'Good pass, son! Go on Soo Fy, go on, lad . . . go on . . . yes, Soo Fy . . . yes . . . YESSSSS!!! YOU CLEVER LITTLE ORIENTAL BASTARD, YOU'RE A LITTLE YELLOW GENIUS!

- That goal you scored was amazing

- Like Liam Brady

- I think you're gonna be in the team for ever now

- Liam Brady plays for Arsenal

- Mr Nolan said I did alright

- Arsenal's the English team my dad chose

- Mr Nolan said I'm a defender so I should never go over the half-way line and whenever I get the ball I should just boot it. 'BOOT IT!!' He shouts 'JUST BOOT IT!!!'

- We don't have football teams like that in Hong Kong. Our food's better though

- Mr Nolan says I booted good today but I'm not as good as my brother – you

- Do you want to come to my house and eat Chinese food?

- Okay

'Chinese

'Japanese

'Dirty knees

'What are these?'

'Is that the other team then?'

'Fucking hell, they're all fucking Chinese!'

'Watch they don't do kung fu on you'

- It was horrible and cold today

- Siu Fai /

- But at least we won

- Siu Fai /

- That run down the left I made worked out

- Siu Fai /

- When the boy on the other team tackled me the ball broke nicely for Adam to score

- Siu Fai /

- What was that name he called me as he tackled me?

- ...

- Ch ... Ch ... something

- It wasn't very nice

- Do you want to come to my house and eat Chinese food?

- Siu Fai, I can't be friends with you no more

I used to feel lonely

I used to long for someone else

Like me

But you're not really like me because we're from different places and different worlds and different atmospheres. But we almost look the same so that works. And you're maybe the kindest funniest sweetest kid I've met. You'd give me the shirt off your back if I was cold. And you're brilliant at football. And you do actually know a bit of kung fu. Because you grew up watching the films, you said.

Everything about you is awesome.

But I can't be friends with you

Because

It was bad when it was just me and all the other kids took the piss out of me all day and I stood out like noodles in a sausage factory but now there's two of us it's even worse we're like bright bamboo dayglo to them everywhere we go they make shit jokes about us teaming up to take over the world like those nasty villains that white men play in silly make-up to make them look Chinese and some people even think we're siblings but we're so different because I'm me and you're you and we're nothing like each other and I'm not even properly Chinese I'm only half and half so that makes me feel all wrong and I just want to blend out and fit in and not stand out and with you I stand out

We

Stand Out

There's no safety in numbers

Sorry

And you're moving to North London soon cuz your dad bought a take-away there

I hope you get to watch Arsenal and meet Liam Brady

Have a nice life

Bye

'Chinese

'Japanese

'Dirty knees

'What are these?'

I dreamed I was a Chinese kid with a Chinese friend at school

Or am I a Chinese kid with a Chinese friend dreaming that I'm not really Chinese and I don't have a Chinese friend?

Was it that formative experience with the Dao of Exclusion and Hate and Racist Violence and Almost Love which drove me here today?

To the screaming tarmac of the thoroughfare out of the Great Capital City of . . .

Well. It's a long way from Xiangyang . . .

Cloud & Obscure #1 云与晦涩 #一

– Master Obscure?

– You must be the one called Cloud

– I came a long way, y' know

– You're very intrepid, Cloud

– I mean, what is this place? Zone 5? Zone 6?

– The journey to the suburbs begins with a single over-priced ticket from a privatised rail franchise

– You're a . . . sage. Right?

– I've been around

– Everyone says. You're a sage. And you're . . . Obscure

– And you're a Cloud

– But you're a Sage

– If you like

– Second only to Pangu I heard

– What do you know about Pangu?

– Pangu was a Sage. And you're a Sage

– 'Virtuosity is undermined by getting a good name for it'

– See, this is what I'm talking about!

– 'A good name is most essentially a way for people to defeat each other and conscious understanding is most essentially a weapon of war'

– What is . . . 'Dao'

– You want to know about Dao

– More than anything

– Why?

- To Make Sense
- Of what?
- My life. My times. My . . . butterfly dreams
- You wanted to ask Pangu
- I couldn't find Pangu
- Well . . . originally 'Dao' meant 'roadway'
- Where does it come from?
- The Pole Star. Via the Milky Way. An Abyss – she is the forbear of myriad things
- Does it lead somewhere?
- If it did that would mean it has a goal
- There's no goal?
- The Dao is formed by walking it
- Physically?
- Whatever we think of as a train and not a car, an object of beauty as opposed to ugliness, or whatever some might decide was strange, grotesque, uncanny, deceptive . . . there is a Dao that opens them into each other, colliding them into a oneness
- So there's . . . loads of different . . . Daos?
- The Dao of ancient kings, the Dao of Heaven, the Dao of all-inclusive love, the Dao of filial piety, the Dao of celebrity, the Dao of grassroots community work, the Dao of free market economics, the Dao of universal basic income, the Dao of Civil / Society Organising –
- That's definitely a Dao /
- The Dao of Confucius and the Dao of Mozi
- The one I heard about is the Dao of non-doing

- Then be free of purpose
- I do have a purpose though
- You have an inner capitalist
- I need to achieve something / yes
- But you wish to cultivate the Dao of non-doing
- I do
- Then you say you want to . . . do
- I really want to . . . do . . . / something
- But the Dao of non-doing is to '*Not* Do'
- But is not wanting to '*Not* Do' wanting to . . . 'Do'?
- Cheeky little fucker aren't you
- Sorry
- No no, anything that bucks the stereotype
- I want to 'Do'. Achieve. Then. After. '*Not* Do'
- You want your *jaozi* 饺子 and you want to eat it
- I don't know what that means but yeah
- So before you retire into Non-Doing /
- Before I kick back / yeah
- What is it you want to . . . do?
- . . .
- . . .
- I want to write the definitive British Chinese Story
- . . .
- . . .
- Such a thing is possible?

- I think the British Chinese Community are crying out for a definitive British Chinese Story

- All of them?

- Do you think I could find it by following a Dao?

- All things are possible. With the Dao

- So what do I . . . do or . . . not do?

- You cultivate your *De* 德

- This is getting really confusing /

- *De* 德 is your 'Virtuosity'

- What the fuck is that?

- If the Dao is like a sort of 'course'. 'Virtuosity' is what you get by completing the course. Or The Dao

- Like a kind of certificate?

- But it's not a piece of paper, you leaden literalist

- What then?

- We're talking here about the virtuosity of the non-deliberate Dao of the world, like innate . . . skill, inborn virtuosity . . . what we do with no . . . actual . . . effort

- Yeah, effort sucks

- Dao 道 and De 德. Say them

- My Chinese is shit

- Your virtuosity is what matters

OBSCURE SINGS

The purest seed of the purest Dao

Vague and dark, dark and vague

Empyreal reach of Ideal Dao

Dull and still, still and dull

Stay still embrace your spirit

Outside you'll straighten with it

Stay still and stay pure

No labour now for cure

Not messing with the seed of your vitality

And then you'll live perennially

When the eye and ear

Won't see or hear

And the mind knows nothing

With nothing clear

Your spirit's that imponderable

Must cleave hard to make comparable

Your mortal body's length of life

Be wary of what's within you

Close yourself to what's outside you

Cuz all this knowledge gonna blunt your vibe

–   Go on then

–   Go . . . on?

–   Your story. Your Definitive British Chinese Story

I got very good grades at school

I suppose that was drummed into me by my *Ma* and *Ba*

Not saying my mum's a tiger mum but . . . 'you need to work hard and do well at school so you can get a good job or I will hit you with this feather duster, you useless fat lazy child'

Ma had a big slipper. It was bigger than *Ma*'s arm. We think *Ma* must have got it from a Tibetan Yeti. I mean, a big Chinese ye– . . . anyway, *Ma* never wore the slipper. She just beat us with it. *Ma* would beat us so hard that we would scream and cry and bleed and have bruises. And *Ma* had watched so many martial arts movies that she would make the noises while she hit us with the slipper. Like –

GNAAAAAAAAARRRRRR! THWACK!!!

HUUUUAAAARRRRRRRR! PUK!!!!

AIIIIIIIIIIYYYYEEEEEEEEEE! HUP!

HYAR! HYAR! HYAR! OOOOO!!!

I think if any of your Western parents beat us like *Ma* did they would be arrested by the child welfare police but we Chinese don't need to bother about any child welfare police because we are always so well-behaved and quiet and we are very stoic and inexpressive so you can hit us as much as you like it really doesn't matter.

I'm only joking

My mum's much nicer than that

And on Sunday, *Ba* would take us for dim sum

And I was always top of the class did my homework ahead of time and home by eight and I never argued with *Ma* and *Ba* never ever ever and the only trouble I ever caused at school was when I opened my lunch box to eat my smelly Chinese food / –

   –   Your mum never made / you Chinese food –

–   / and the smell went everywhere and all the British kids and even the British teachers would look over and make remarks about how smelly my food was but I was always so good at maths / –

   –   This is really / good but –

–   / and science but not history because I was told that's of no use to a Chinese person / –

   –   I don't believe / it –

- / - and I was always home by eight and never ever argued with *Ma* and *Ba* / –

- -Stop /

- / - and I was quite popular with the other British kids because I could help them with their homework and I was always home by eight / –

- -I don't believe / you –

- / - and all the British teachers liked me because I was always polite and respectful to them because I was taught to be / –

- -I don't believe / you–

- / - respectful to my elders because that's part of our culture so there was never any trouble no / –

   - **STOP**

- I joined the Conservative Party but I'm not political they just seemed like the most sensible and not dangerous and radical plus they have the best networking opportunities /

   - Oh fuck off

   - What???

   - I don't believe you

   - You don't . . .?

   - No

   - None of it?

   - Not one word

   - But . . . I need to conform /

   - Find your virtuosity /

   - To the standard /

- Find your virtu /
- Be definitive /
- Your virtuosity
- My . . .
- *De*. 德. Virtuosity
- . . .
- . . .
- Here I go

Virtuosity (*De* 德)

I crush the powder in spoon hot water and sponge

Place the needle in the centre and pull that plunge

Sucking chemical fluid through the barrel inside

As I tighten that belt, strap in for the ride

My arms are torn and scarred and swollen

From this habit I fuel with goods I've stolen

Cicatrix tissue so hard to pierce

But the spike of that rig is sharp and fierce

As the rush washes up from my toes to my brain

White light, white heat gonna drive me insane

My soul leaves my body and floats stone free

And samples all the things I yearn to be . . .

Acerbic mystic, holistic heuristic, indirect rustic, metronomic drumstick, bottom-dweller, fortune-teller, high-flyer, sky-pyre, unassuming rebel, self-consuming seashell, abstruse jester, danseuse ester, frivolous sage and voice of the age

By –

Enlivening confusions, enlightening illusion, taunting misdirections, flaunting rhythm section, with surreal grotesquery, free-wheel accessory, perspicacious satire, curvilinear high wire, virtuoso reasonings, arioso sweetening, insouciant despair, noncomforming fanfare, mischievous fallacies, rejection of reality, morbid exuberance, talkative protuberance, impudent jokes and marijuana smoke, enfolding encipher and jolting non-sequitur

In fact, I'd like to have <u>been</u> a non-sequitur

Especially a jolting non-sequitur

I'd like to have been Zhuangzi

But all I had was grandiose dreams

And not Butterfly Dreams . . .

And you try taking an LSD trip with Benny Hill on prime-time imitating your dad

And you try faking a carefree rip with the kids in the playground deprecating your dad

Hong Kong Phooey on a school day Fu Manchu on Sunday

Chop suey is your nickname Dr Who got yellowface

'Grasshopper' they shout like The Sage To David Carradine

'n saying your sister must 'a been an emperor's concubine

They're pulling their eyes like they'll do themselves an injury

Self-inflicted pain so they can take the piss and pillory

And when you fight back against the bullies by the bike shed

They medicate your senses 'cuz you started it Mike said

You're removed from class like an antisocial element

To school the half-caste to perform less malevolent

They say just rise above it an' learn to take the joke

Whilst they swap their rs for ls an' gurn and gloat

In this tolerant land of meantime not Greenwich

Where you try to play guitar and they call you Yellow Hendrix

The only yellow I got was jaded junkie jaundice

When I tried to get mellow like a faded flunkie corpus

On a sofa in a council house in rural-urban hell

Athenian pull to extend that spell

You wipe the blood from your arm and fix for outdoors

In that twenty-four-seven of always needing more

You smash the window of the car and you grab what you can

No *Oceans 11* just crowbar and scram

Forcing open cash-tills an' fleeing them alarms

That siren sound flashing light that means you harm

In the store Pringle sweaters are stuffed inside a jacket

As you walk don't run with the girth of this racket

Sometimes you get chased and assaulted and hit

You can't get away you're not fit for this shit

You're caught in the sewer of the capitalist system

In the harsh social order of Keynesian wisdom

The sergeant in the station sneers at your state

Says you'll be dead real soon that's your miserable fate

You try to be defiant but you're beaten inside

That hole in your soul opens up so wide . . .

You took the car 'cuz you were sick, couldn't walk to the
supplier

After you'd robbed the stereo and technical appliance

Wasn't subtle or aesthetic you just grabbed and ripped

Cursing and swearing 'cuz you needed that fix

So you made that fateful choice that night to take their car

If you'd walked you'd be cool and it really wasn't far

But your Dao and your De got corrupted in this instance

An' you allowed cupidity to blur your resistance

The Material World and its tantalization

Of wheels and hubcaps and acceleration

Has dazzled up your senses and corrupted your vision

Besides you're fucking knackered from street-life attrition

You fired the ignition 'cuz the keys were inside (believe!)

You revved up the engine and you took it for a ride

You cruised round the block like a plastic gangster

Feeling all large like a supreme mansur

You were so hyped up you didn't see the public payphone

STOP: YES, THIS IS A PERIOD DRAMA. CONTINUE:

You were so hyped up you didn't see the public payphone

At the corner right where you took that Ford and roamed

Inside the owner and his bestie are calling the feds

As you drive by their faces turn red

Like the colour of the phone-box which was BT trad

Their countenance is glowering 'cuz you made them so mad

Into his friend's jalopy piles the victim of your crime

And on your tail they fly in double-quick time

The first thing that alerts you in the rear-view mirror

Is their angry flashing lights getting nearer and nearer

You panic and you floor it at high-speed down

The narrow winding roads of this dead-end town

Which are nothing like the boulevards in Hollywood movies

Which are vast and wide and car-chase groovy

Made for screeching wheels and stunt-drive chaos

Whereas here in the sticks it's just pent-up pathos

Taking corners at 90 risking life and limb

Skidding and sliding as the tyres they spin

You don't believe in God but you're offering Hail Mary

Praying please Holy Mother this is getting kind of scary

Then you burn your luck and you hit a cul-de-sac

You're forced to flee the car and they're screaming 'you're a maniac!'

They chase you on foot through the lanes of the estate

While your chest explodes with your pounding pulse rate

You're aching inside and struggling to breathe

Thinking fake it to make it and hopef'ly deceive

Your pursuers into thinking you're a champion athlete

When the only thing that's fast and fit's your racing heartbeat

And truth be told your ruse it nearly pays off

No Sun Tzu ploy but it almost shakes off

The maddened CB handle and his wheezing pal

Whose stamina fades along with their morale

You take another corner and you think you've 'scaped

But shock an' horror, a brick wall is in your way

There's nowhere left to hide you're there right for the taking

They're sore as hell and you're gonna get a beating

You're a lover not a fighter but this is self-preservation

You look around for a weapon to defend you from vexation

The only thing at hand is a rusty metal dustbin

You try to lift it up but you're straining like a has-been

'Cuz you've only been taking the wrong kind of steroid

Which ravaged your muscles and left you destroyed

But you try and lift this thing to throw at your assailants

Who stand back wide-eyed in perplexed surveillance

You heave and launch but the best that you can manage

Is a drop on the concrete where it does no damage

Just makes a kind of clang then a sorrowful groan

As it rolls around the pavement like an aimless stone

Your captors are emboldened now and start to close in

There's nowhere left to run to your enormous chagrin

You close your eyes and sigh and wait for retribution

'cuz you're a six-stone weakling who needs a blood transfusion

So what do you do?

There was nothing to do

And in that moment I found myself thinking

Zhuangzi

What would the sage say?

But Zhuangzi hated sages

He blamed the sages for all the problems of the world

Maybe that's why I'm a drug addict

Because of the sages

And Zhuangzi would probably say something about

Virtuosity

Here

Now

In this back alley in a rural-provincial town where a physically depleted mad-eyed dreamer was about to be kicked senseless by two angry white men over a stolen car . . .

Ballad of Virtuosity (De 德) 精湛的歌谣

Virtuosity

Virtuosity

Feng and Huang are Phoenix

Yin and Yang's collective thesis

From the ashes in the West

In the East creation's quest

But you lost your virtuosity

Your former grandiosity

The future is away from you

And it will never wait for you

It's a long long long

Way on the wind

It's all wrong wrong wrong

That song you sing

(But who am I to say)

Virtuosity

Virtuosity

When the Dao is in this world

The sage lives by its De

When the Dao has left this dream

The sage still flows the stream

Good fortune is a feather

You can't carry it forever

Trouble weighs more than this earth

It's weighed from day of birth

It's a long long long

Way on the wind

It's all wrong wrong wrong

That song you sing

(But who am I to say)

You impress the rest and oppress their request to address their behest to access the test of what invests the best

With your Virtuosity

Let it all go!

The line's too straight you can walk it but not talk it or unlock it or unblock it those brambles and thorns gonna tangle and scorn

Your Virtuosity

Let it all go!

You need a zig-zag stride a wig-wag ride a sight-gag slide a ragbag guide that won't impede your steps in this cosmic mess

Of your Virtuosity

Keep your feet unharmed!

And it's a long long long

Way on the wind

It's all wrong wrong wrong

That song you sing

(But who am I to say)

Christianity 基督教

. . . I'll just start by saying thanks for having me on the podcast, Team ESEA. First of all, I just knew it was that classic Chinese parent narrative they wanted, you know, 'got very good grades at school, be a doctor . . . or a lawyer . . . something that earns good money . . . this is their country, we're just foreigners here . . .'

And on Sundays *Ba* would take us for dim sum

- Are you telling big fat fibs again, you little oriental Beezlebub?

- Father McNamara!

- Yes, me, you quince-coloured fabulist

- What are you doing here in my Definitive British Chinese Story?

Father McNamara was the priest in the church next to my Catholic school. There was a headmaster at the school. Or headmistress. I don't remember which. Or maybe I deliberately de-gendered the Head Person or Head Human because I want my story to be inclusive. Father McNamara though. Father McNamara was definitely a Man. And despite the gender-non-specific Head Teacher, Father McNamara actually ran that little Catholic school in the heart of that rural-provincial-urban-city-town that was the space for my coming of age

But I digress

- Father McNamara. What you doing here?

- Bringing some much-needed truth and integrity to this woke trite box-ticking trash you're attempting to trot out here

- But it's my story, Father McNamara

- And the Lord detests lying lips

- How . . . how do you know I'm lying???

- That bit about the dim sum

- 'And on Sundays *Ba* would take us for dim sum' /

- Your dad couldn't order dim sum from a picture menu

- But I've got to make my story definitive / –

- Your mum's not even Chinese /

- The Definitive British Chinese Story / –

- The only thing that's definitive about you is that chip on your shoulder

- But, sir /

- Don't call me 'sir'

- Sorry, sir. I mean, Father

- I'm a priest for Christ sakes

- Yes, Father

- Why don't you like calling me 'Father'?

- Maybe I don't want to be a Christian, sir. Father

- Why not?

- I'm Chinese, Father

- Jesus loves everyone

- Even Chinese?

- Even . . . don't try and catch me out, you little Pharisee

- I mean, I'm Chinese. Well, I'm half . . . Chinese. How do you know I'm not into Buddhism or Communism or all kinds of weird stuff. Sir?

- Your parents sent you to this school, it's a Catholic school, they want you to be a good Catholic, your mum told me

- My mum's not Chinese though, Father

- Your father nodded when she said

- My father nods at everything . . . Father. I mean, I wouldn't take my father's nodding as a necessary sign of enthusiasm, Father. Because, Father, my father wasn't born here, Father, my father was born somewhere in Asia, Father, my father is very conscious that he has a Chinese accent, Father, and it makes him feel inadequate and strange, Father, so my father's quiet most of the time, Father, except when he loses his temper, Father, when he chucks things around and smashes up the house . . . Father. See this is why I don't like calling you 'Father', Father. It gets confusing . . . Father

- So it was your father who made your front tooth look like a crucifix / then?

- That's a sensitive subject and I'd rather not go there just yet / Father

- So you inherit your temper from your father?

- Inherited racial trauma, Father. Except I don't know that terminology yet so I'll just nod and say 'maybe, Father'

- He's a Chinaman, your father?

- . . .

- Your father's a Chinaman?

- On Sunday, *Ba* would take us for dim sum /

- I thought we'd established that / wasn't the case

- On Sunday / –

- By the Pope's / ferula!
- *Ba* would take us for / dim sum
- No he never /
- ON SUNDAY. *BA* WOULD TAKE US FOR DIM SUM

Asian Parent Song 亚洲父母之歌

NO HE FUCKING NEVER!!!!

Daddy wasn't dai lo

Mummy was a gwai poh

They couldn't speak a word of Cantonese

Never got an ang pao

Daddy didn't know how

The only thing we had was dirty knees

I'm not obedient I'm not dutiful

Mummy was lenient daddy's not inscrutable

They got drunk and laughed at Benny Hill

They smoked skunk and took prescription pills

We didn't have no subtle Asian trait

I didn't draw no Lucky Number Eight

No cultural haven from the daily race hate

My face was subtle but it had some Asian traits

Sweet 'n' sour pork balls

Holidays in Cornwall

We lived like a 70s sitcom

Though we tried to act dumb

We were like a sore thumb

Something like a racial stink bomb

Never went to Asia or the Chinese supermarket

No fatt choy we were in a different orbit

Never had a hot pot or feasted on a roast duck

The only thing that I got's a pudding basin haircut
We weren't subtle and we had no Asian traits
I didn't draw no Lucky Number Eight
No cultural haven from the daily race hate
My face was subtle but it had some Asian traits

The First Time I Went To Chinatown 我去唐人街的第一次

And I was on a college day trip to London the first time I went to Chinatown

And the teacher takes us through Chinatown

> I think my college friends are actually quite scared

> – *Where's this then?*

> – *They're all Chinese!*

> – *Are we in China?*

We're in Chinatown I say

> Trying to sound like I knew what I was talking about

Trying to sound like

> I'm at Home

And the people there do look a bit like me I suppose but they look more like my dad and my grandma but even then they aren't quite the same

> I want to be at Home

I have no Home

> I want my People

I have no People

I think I went in a bakery there to buy a bun

> I look hard at the lady serving me as she hands me the bun and takes my money then gives me the change

I looked hard for recognition

> For a sense of

Familiarity

> But there's nothing

None at all

> It's like I've come Home but my Family don't recognize me

Like all those years in the playground being baited by white kids –

> *'Chinese*
>
> *'Japanese*
>
> *'Dirty knees*
>
> *'What are these'*

I'd wished with everything I had that I wouldn't stand out and I wouldn't look Chinese anymore so I wouldn't get called chink and China and grasshopper and Kendo and slant-eyes and spring roll and Tenko and gook /

> If you believe hard enough your dreams come true

I had a dream where I wasn't Chinese any more

> Or am I not Chinese and dreaming I'm Chinese and wanting to not look Chinese

Because that was the difference

> And here I am buying a bun from a Chinese lady in a bakery hoping she would notice I was Chinese

And she'll smile at me and recognize me and know me and

> Accept me

But she doesn't

> She looks straight through me

Nothing

> Says thank you then smiles at the next customer and speaks to her in a language I don't know how to speak

> > *'Chinese*
> >
> > *' Japanese*
> >
> > *'None of these*
> >
> > *'A lonely tree'*

Christianity 2.0 基督教

- You cannot

- I know /

- You cannot inflict these tales of Sodom and Gomorrah on / people

- I warned you, Father. But you wouldn't listen, Father

- It's . . . too whimsical

- I'm adrift in a racial landscape, Father

- You're what?

- I was trying to be poetic, Father. It's another fancy concept I picked up later on in life from a complimentary review, Father

- But we need to see your rage and trauma, child

- I'm not sure anyone's interested in the rage and trauma of Chinese people, Father. I'm not sure Chinese people are even interested in the rage and trauma of Chinese people / Father

- Well you need to find your audience, you Mongolian Moloch

- What does that mean?

- You need to know who this story is **for**

- But I'm . . . a pimple on the backside of Multicultural Britain, Father, I don't fit any / where

- So you're trying be subtle. Less confrontational. Less on the nose

- Sounds just like being Chinese to me

- Turning the other cheek?

- I haven't got any cheeks left to turn though, Father. I'm all out of cheeks. In case you didn't notice. I'm at the point where all my cheeks have been slapped as red raw as slabs of beef and are hanging off my face like vaginal curtains, Father

—   Sufferance!

—   Is that what Jesus would've done, Father?

—   You're not Jesus

—   No. I'm Chinese. Kind of

—   So you keep saying though I'd question how 'Chinese' you actually are. I mean, what does that word even mean, son? It comes from the word 'Qin' I think which was the first state to unify the entirety of the individual countries of the central plains of what we now call 'China' / –

—   Fuuuuck /

—   with the kind of iron hand authoritarian patriarchy that makes my milquetoast Catholicism look positively progressive / let me tell you

—   Father McNamara, are you schooling me on my own Chinese culture?

—   You know as much about Chinese culture as a fish knows about tap dancing, you fauxlebrity fakester / –

—   This is fucking outrageous / –

—   This is the magic of theatre, kiddo, you can play with conventions and be mischievous with form and narrative and generally whacky and experimental in a way that'll get all those hipster theatre bloggers singing your praise

—   Well, you can if you're White and university educated, Father /

—   I'm gonna pretend I never heard / that

—   Convenient /

–   and move on to say that . . . being that we have
    absolutely no conventional chronological structure here,
    we – that is myself and the audience – would like to
    segue neatly to the time even before you met this Sui Fai
    and went to school and got called names every day

–   You heard the Sui Fai / story

–   Bit sentimental for my Heiner Müller Frank Castorf civic
    disobedience theatre tastes but / there we go

–   Has someone spiked the theatre water cooler? /

–   we – that is the audience and myself / –

–   You're speaking on behalf of the entire / audience

–   would like to see The Curious Incident of the Forward
    Maxillary Incisor

–   That's . . . sensitive. I told you /

–   Showbiz isn't for snowflakes or butterflies, kid /

–   But mental health and well / being –

–   **Are you or are you not a fearless story-teller???**

–   . . .

–   So, without further ado, ladies & gentlemen, boys & girls
    (and those who haven't made up their mind yet) Young
    Cloud here is going to give you . . . what d'you call it
    again?

–   The Dao of the Tooth

Dao Of The Tooth 牙之道

I guess I'll tell you the tale of my tooth

The one situated at the front

Ever since I was five it's given me ruth

In fact it's been a bit of a / cunt –

    –   continuing yam, a didactic jam

A fable of morality

Written in pain and blood book slam

And banal brutality

It was a gift from a kid whose name I don't recall

Who fixed me in a permanent way

Now this particular toy was heavy as fuck

A kid's version of an automobile

Three feet long, more like a truck

It might as well been made of steel

I was lying down enjoying the sun

On that blissful summer's day

    –   *What you doing, ching chong?*

    –   Please don't call me that

    –   *I'll call you what I like, ning nong*

    –   Are you . . . a racist?

    –   *I'm a five-year-old kid with the Great British Sense Of Humour, ting tong*

    –   'The truth is not always beautiful . . .'

    –   *Gimme my toy car back, ling long*

    –   Your toy car's a bit shit tbh

- *What's wrong with my toy car, ping pong*
- I didn't even touch your toy car truth be told
- *Why not, ding dong?*
- It's big
- *That's the point, sing song*
- And . . . unwieldy
- *What the fuck is . . . unwieldy . . . bing bong?*
- 'Conscious understanding emerges from conflict'
- *Oh you wanna fight me, xing xong?*
- 'Give evil nothing to oppose and it will disappear by itself'
- *You . . .*
- *. . .*
- *You . . .*
- *. . .*
- *. . . cheeky Chinese chunker*
- So

What the hell happened next on that fateful day (Rewind Rewind)

What the hell happened next on that fateful day (Rewind Rewind)

What the hell happened next on that fateful day (Rewind Rewind)

What the hell happened next on that fateful day (Rewind Rewind)

- *And why don't we get both sides of the story this time?*

You wanna hear more we gotta go to four-four

You wanna hear more we gotta go to four-four

I don't remember that day, I just might
Remember it well for the rest of my days

I remember you standing up there
Struggling to raise that four-wheel chaise
I remember your arrogant wit
You were never fazed

All high and based

You're Oriental, I try to forget ever seeing your face
Your inferior race
Almond eyes in a wu tang brace
And when you said 'Hi', I forgot my dang name
'Cuz I was feeling pain, you were to blame
I assuaged my shame

You're like me, you never learned to cry

I'm sure I don't know what you mean
You jumped-up little gook
Just like me, you never found the Dao
I'm getting shook
Calling me names really ain't how

My name is adopted English –
My dad's an immigrant
Where's your family from?

A colony, six thousand miles away

I won't accept I won't accept

So so so so

So this is what it feels like when they won't take shit
When they think they're at your level! My supremacy hit?
Keeps bucking my priv'lege, talkin' 'bout Dao
When I jus' squint and say Nee Hao
And be Mean Chow

The conversation lasted two minutes, maybe three minutes
All the kid said was flip disagreement, made
Me scream and do an angry dance
At the kid's posture, egotistical stance. They're an
Insolent chink, I gave 'em a chance

I asked about fam'ly, did you see the kid's answer?
Slant eyes all defiant, already askance?
The gimp's clueless, really should be shitting their pants

Bumptious, lying in the sun
Hubris, boy am I triggered
I wanna put the kid back in their place
'Cuz I'm pissed and I really lost face I need a
Victim
I lift up the car

Vindictive
It's three feet long
Afflictive
It weighs a fucking ton

Your frontal middle tooth this plaything will enshrine
My dental plaque?
I'm about to change your life
Why are you raising that fake Cadillac
I'm Number One!
White boy in a world in which
My shade is the only thing that's rich
My pride was stung by your mouth
So Imma make your Taiwan face head south
'Cuz I'm the baddest and the shittiest and my rage isn't witty it's
invidious
The heaviness of this thing is insidious

Ha? What you doing up there like Atlas?

Revenge,

I'm taking revenge

Against who?

Well I'll tell you . . .

Against YOU!

I'm after you 'cuz you're a lippy fucker
I intend to brain you with this lump

Of metal that weighs like a fire pump
Believe me I intend to throw it in your ming mong mug
But there's a stump
It's too heavy and my arms they slump
So I drop it on your face 'cuz I am stumped

I see it coming

I watch it leave my hands and fall through the air

Like a meteor

It hits my teeth!

The lump of metal lands on China kid's head
Ha, your blood's like mine it's not yellow it's red
It flows all down your mien that in my prejudice state
I chose to hate
The hate I sate
Try'na bait

Why you in my grill, making me remember this?
It's no big deal, you went and saw a dentist
Who fixed your tooth real quickly, I'm certain it's all fine
We should move on, I drew the line

So my tooth
My tooth
My tooth
My tooth
My whole life
My life (learn to cry)
My life (learn to cry)
My life (learn to cry)

But the dentist
The dentist
The dentist
The dentist
The dentist will provide
Will provide (learn to cry)
Will provide (learn to cry)

Will provide (learn to cry)
All the solace, you require
The dentist will provide
Will provide
Will provide

Learn to cry
Learn to cry
Learn to cry
Learn to cry
Don't you ever remind
My tooth will always remind

To the dentist!!!

And all the solace he'll provide

An' all free on the NHS

All free on the NHS

WAIT STOP

THIS IS A PERIOD DRAMA

CONTINUE

Novocaine Dreams 诺卡因之梦

So what with the rage pills they prescribed to stop me
getting triggered by racial abuse . . .

'Chinese

'Japanese

'Dirty knees

'What are these?'

. . . and the novocaine the dentist pumped into me with a
needle the size of an elephant's leg it's like I rolled in
strawberry fields forever under the sky with diamonds in a
purple haze and skipped the light fandango before I ever
even knew about these things . . .

'Chinese

'Japanese

'Twisted tooth

'Wasted youth'

Laying back in that dentist's chair

I had a trip that's really rare

I didn't meet no sage or teller of truth

But I had a scene

With my front tooth

On that x-ray screen

As I cried forsooth

Hey kid

You

I know

You're a

I know

You're

I know

YOU'RE A TOOTH

Incisorive isn't it

I'm sorry I'm off my face and I'll find out one day that when you take LSD and ketamine and magic mushrooms or ayahuasca in a jungle in Peru you might just meet God but this is right here right now live and direct five years old wasted on dentist gear and I'm meeting . . . my tooth

Yeah well don't go on too much , you'll use up all my time

Alright, don't get all heavy . . . Tooth

Daya

What was that

I forgot, you can't speak Chinese

What does that mean?

It means Big Tooth

That's kind of what I said

Don't be pedantic

You're the one who's being being pedantic, you orthodontic tyrant

Just shut up and listen to me okay

Okay

It's like this

This dentist here, he's gonna rip me out. Don't panic, you'll grow another one, you're still young. But it'll grow all crooked. So they'll

give you a brace. It's supposed to straighten the tooth out. But you've got no patience whatsoever. So you'll chuck the brace in the river and watch it float on the slate-grey surface before a duck or something tries to eat the brace and nearly chokes on plastic and nickel and wire. Don't laugh, it's cruel. Then you'll put up with the crooked molar and the fact your mouth looks like a sixteenth-century graveyard because . . . you're a drug-addled waster, what do you care, but then one day you're gonna get all clean and sober and have fancy ideas about being some kind of Shakespeare actor and the drama school will insist you get your teeth straightened and another dentist will say you need a crown so the crooked tooth gets lopped off to a stub and you get a shiny new crown put in but all the time that stump of a crooked tooth that a racially aggravated kid gave you will be rotting away and rotting away . . .

It's there to remind you

*I'm **gone** to remind you*

My time's up they're ripping me out

Take care kid

Gettin' loosened from my gum now
I believe I'm fixin' to die . . .

I coulda last fo'ever
But today's my last one here

***AAAARRRRGGGHHHEEEEYYYYAAARRRGGGHHH
HEEEEEOOOOOHHHHHARRRRGGGHHH!!!***

. . .

That was . . . Horrible

Why, Father McNamara? Or are you Master Obscure? Why did you make me relive that paean of pain that was

My poor tooth

Gone

Just thrown in the bin all covered in blood and gore and gum while I float on the numbing cloud of

A Novocaine Dream

Where I'm a butterfly

With a straight tooth that's never been messed with by a racist

Or am I . . .

. . .

> *My Ba. My **father**. He was a man of very few words. Just like they show on the TV. He never spoke really. In fact I don't remember him saying one word. Ever. Not one. And he never smiled. Or laughed. Or cried. In fact his face never moved. Not once. Not even an inch. I sometimes wondered if Ba was made of plastic*
>
> *But on Sunday Ba would take us for dim sum*

Cloud & Obscure #2 云与晦涩 #二

- I actually wanted to know what would happen next. It's been a long time since I've felt that

- I'm flattered, Master Obscure. But it's too obscure

- What's obscure?

- That story, Master Obscure. It's not . . . definitive

- The unifying narrative, Cloud?

- I have to find my target market

- The Yellow Emperor ordered the world by making the hearts and minds of the people focus on unity

- Unity! Yes, we need unity / –

- The Yellow Emperor focused the people on unity so much that when somebody didn't cry at the death of a loved one, or the loss of history, or the end of truth, that was seen as a good thing

- With Virtuosity, I can . . . find my audience, my . . . place

- Why do you want to do this, Acolyte Cloud?

- I want to . . . Represent. Representation . . . Matters

- . . .

- Isn't that what Pangu believed?

- Pangu . . . created

- I want to create

- You want to compete, Cloud

OBSCURE *sings*

Tree Song 树歌

I'd rather be

A useless tree

And grow here for millennia

I'd rather see

The birds and bees

No people here forever

If you have use

They'll use you up

And they won't remember

They sapped your juice

And filled their cup

After you're dismembered

I'd rather be

A useless tree

- Cloud

- Master Obscure

- Why don't you tell me what happened after you stole the car?

- If you're sure that's . . .

  On Sunday, Ba would take us for dim sum . . .

No

On this particular Sunday I awoke to the clanging of metal doors and jangling of keys on the plastic mattress and itchy blanket of the hard wooden bench that was the sole furnishing in my own personally allocated cell of the local

constabulary police station of the rural-urban town I
misspent my youth in

And there I met him

The Sage Of The Law

Actually I met him many times . . .

The Dao of Legalism 法家之道

– Fucking state of you, tosser

– Sergeant Harris. I knew I could rely on your empathetic nature

– Your parents must wonder what they did to deserve you, you absolute fucking waste of seminal fluid

– Whereas yours must bless the day they brought such a ray of human kindness into the world

– You leave my parents out of this, you little wanker

– Actually 'human kindness' gets emphasised too much, according to Zhuangzi

– What the fuck are you on about now, you little tea leaf?

– Zhuangzi, Sergeant Harris. He was an ancient Chinese sage. See, you can use the act of indication of the unindicated that belongs to all indication. But that's really no match for using the unindicated itself as the indication of the unindicated that belongs to all indication

– . . .

– Something is allowed because some allowing of it has happened. The Dao is formed by walking it, Sergeant Harris

– . . .

– And someone who can maintain the Dao. Within the darkest dark alone that person sees daybreak, Sergeant Harris

– You fucking mad little cunt

– Strong malice is often no different to strong human kindness, Sergeant. Both seek to alter the world and both can have serious consequences

- Yeah. Whatever. Surprised those two whose car you nicked didn't kick the living shit out of you when they caught you

- I think they were both too done in after chasing me through the estate. All that adrenalin, Sarge. We're not used to it like you with your Starsky and Hutch lifestyle

- Cheeky little twat

- The Dao of plastic coffee cups and stale bacon sandwiches. Some of us lack this requisite Virtuosity

- Look at it this way, they wouldn't have got no grief off me if they'd Japanese smack-shacked you till you had a hole in your chest, you mismanaged little bag of bones

- I can imagine that's one bit of supposedly criminal behaviour you'd have positively applauded, Sergeant Harris

- Druggie dregs like you don't deserve the protection of laws

- Can I ask you a question?

- I ask the questions here, Bruce

- This is a really even-handed universe you live in isn't it /

- You're in a police station and I'm the fucking police, you ponce, you do what I say when I say it how I say it the way I say it and if I wanna get gangster on your pock-ridden arse I fucking well will. You keep giving me lip I'll stomp a mudhole in you, skeletor saddo. There. That's my Dao. It's the Dao of the Cunt. Deal with it, syrup head

- I'm genuinely curious though. Every time I get nicked–

- Oh you're curious /

- I am /

- Well, **I'm** curious, runty

– About . . . what?

– How comes you get to talk all proper an' about proper Chinese stuff like Dao and Zhu . . . Zhu . . . Zhu /

– / Zhuangzi

– Zhuangzi, yeah. 'Cuz you're an uneducated little pillock. You dropped out of school when you was twelve basically. An' the only thing that's Chinese about you is your dad, your ugly Ming The Merciless mug and your pudding bowl haircut, you little twat

– I'm gonna have to let you in on a secret, Sergeant Harris

– . . .

– We're in a play. We're in my play. The play that's the story of my life

– . . .

– . . .

– You getting all meta-theatre on me, oolong tea-leaf?

– I'm . . . look, you're in my play and you're part of my . . . narrative

– Don't I get my own narrative?

– No you fucking don't /

– Fuck that

– You can't /

– I can do what the fuck I like, I'm white you're not you're a crim and I'm a cop. There. That's what I call Poetry

– But / –

– And Now. I want My Moment

– Your / . . .

- Yeah. The story of *my* fucking life. 'Cuz it's a fuck sight more interesting than your biased whiny snowflake one-note rant. Far too indignant for subtlety / –

- You nicked that line from one of my less-than-flattering theatre reviews of the future / –

- So fucking what, you ain't even authentic. There's no cultural lens there at all / –

- Another one! You've been reading post-millennial *Time Out Online*, this is meant to be the 1980s / –

- Too right, you out of date little yellow fogey. You're like a bloody *Carry On* film. And why you so obsessed with Dr fucking Who? Chock full of racial stereotypes that is. Fucker might have had the whole of time and space to get round in his factually inaccurate looking police-box but he still dressed up white people as orientals didn't he

- :o

- So. Here's my tale

Fall'n ching chong, to be White is miserable
Doing or Suffering: but of this be sure,
To do ought good never will be our task,
But ever to do ill our sole delight

- What the fuck is this?

- This is your moment, Sergeant Harris. And you're misquoting Milton

- For fuck's sake, why don't you just put a fucking pantomime villain moustache on me. Like fucking Fu Manchu

*Imagine a person, tall, lean and . . . **White**. High-shouldered and . . . **White**. With a brow like Shakespeare and a face like Satan, a close-shaven skull, and the angry, belligerent eyes of the Angry **White** Man. And all this accumulated in one giant **White** Man, with all the resources of a uniform. Imagine that awful being, and you have a mental picture of Sergeant Keith Churchill Harris, the racist **White** copper incarnate*

–   Oh bollocks

As a small boy I embarked on a vendetta tempered with the ideal of justice after swearing vengeance against criminals after witnessing the murder of my beloved parents Thomas and Martha /

–   Sergeant / Harris

I trained himself physically /

–   Sergeant / Harris –

and intellectually, to monitor the Gotham / streets at night

–   That's Batman

–   . . .

*I was bitten by a radioactive spider, and for the last twenty years I thought I was the only **white** Spider-man –*

I stole a TARDIS and escaped from Gallifrey then they regenerated me into a woman . . .

–   You fucking little wanker. I'm stuck in your narrative. I'm a caricature Cishet Toxic White Male

–   Now you know how it feels when someone else writes your story

–   Can I just do one bit? Can I just . . . open my soul?

–   The play's too long as it is, Sergeant Harris

–   At least . . . can't you tell me what happened? To me? This is a Tennessee Williams Memory Play innit?

–   Okay. I only know this. Sergeant Harris . . .

Later when I was in rehab paid for by the Department of Social Services – YesThisIsAPeriodDramaILaterFoundOut ThatMyRouteOrDaoIntoAMiddleClassArtsCareerIsNo LongerAvailableToWorkingClassKidsWithNoMoney BecauseTheArtsIsAnIndulgenceAndReallyNotNecessary WhichIsWhyEtonCollegeHasNotOneButTwoStateOf TheArtTheatres – but I digress. When I was in rehab my mum brought me the local *Evening Chronicle* that carried a small news item that said one Sergeant Keith Churchill Harris was suspended from duty for cannabis use. The news item was small and located on Page 8 but there was a grainy headshot of your bad self. I believe you then had to leave the force in disgrace, Sergeant Harris. Who knows, maybe you struggled for employment after that and sank into a miasma of alcoholism and despair which cost you your marriage and your relationship with your children but maybe just maybe in middle-age you reached out for help and began attending Alcoholics Anonymous meetings where you found sobriety and peace and maybe even love with a man named Jerome you met online. But I can't actually be certain about any of that since my access to newspapers was a bit restricted in the twelve-step treatment centre I was lucky enough to land up in and not even the local news was very interested in the Life and Career of Sergeant Keith Churchill Harris

– Right. Thank you

– Do you need a . . . moment, Sergeant Harris?

– I think we should just get on with the show

– I want to make sure you're getting the support you need

– The . . .

– I mean . . . we take mental health and well-being very seriously, Sergeant

– . . . we?

– We like to think of the theatre as a . . . healing space

– You're a comically deluded little fucker ain't you

– Is there a mental health first-aider in the audience?

– Oh for the love of / cider!

– We probably should've done a sensitivity read / first –

– I'll fucking sensitively read you / in a minute

– and the Arts Council really needs to fund in situ self-care / therapy

– JUST FUCKING GET ON WITH IT, CRETIN

– Well there's no need to be abusive / Sergeant Harris

– Listen, you might be the tone police but I'm the actual police and I say we get back in the liberal echo chamber and get on with the fucking play or so help me I'll stick my boot so far up your ass, the beads of sweat on my leg are gonna quench your thirst

– . . .

– . . .

– Where were we?

– I just called you 'syrup head'

– Oh yeah. And I go :- I'm genuinely curious though. Every time I get nicked –

– Which is all the fucking time –

– (You took the words right of my mouth) every time I get nicked, in you come to . . . share your views and impart some wisdom to me

– . . .

– Why is that, out of interest?

– . . .

– . . .

– Enjoy it while it lasts, Cloudy Cock. You'll be dead in a year's time.

Ma was very strict. Ma would wake us at 4am. We would do calisthenics and tai chi. Then piano and ballet. And Ma would test us on our spelling . . .

And on Sundays, Ba would take us for dim sum

Cloud & Obscure #3 云与晦涩 #三

–   You certainly lasted just a tad longer than the one year
    allotted you by the eminent sage Sergeant Harris

–   Is that . . . an achievement, Master Obscure?

–   When life comes it cannot be refused. When it departs it
    cannot be detained

–   . . .

–   If I may be so linear: what happened after that, Master
    Cloud?

In order to stop medicating myself with nasty street drugs
cut with brick dust and flour because

'Chinese

'Japanese

'Dirty knees

'What are these?'

I was

I was

Racially abused at school

And

'Chinese

'Japanese

'Dirty knees

'What are these?'

I was

I was

Adrift in a racial landscape (you can tell I'm particularly fond of that one). I'm inserting present me into past me . . . or am I past me dreaming of future me?'

They said I needed a spiritual awakening

And a Higher Power

So I said

Can

I

Throw

The

Yijing 易經?

It is the Book Of Changes after all

Perhaps the audience would like to . . .

Audience Participation, anyone?

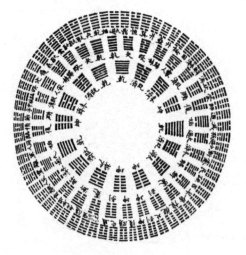

What

What does it mean?

Cloud & Obscure #3 云与晦涩 #三 cont'd

I'd rather be

A useless tree

And grow here for millennia

– Did Pangu understand the *Yijing* 易經, Master
  Obscure?

– . . . The Darkening of the Light . . .

– Do you know what it means?

– Kun . . . Li . . . younger Yin . . .

– Does Virtuosity help you read it?

– Stagnation . . . /

– Can you understand it, Master Obscure?

– 'Heaven over Earth . . .'

– I threw the *Yijing* 易經 the day I left rehab

– How much did it cost you?

– The social security used to pay for rehab in those
  days

– Your story is a period drama, Old Cloud

– Can you understand it?

– The systematic dismantling of our welfare state? No
  not at all /

– I meant the *Yijing* 易经

- No. I can't understand any of it
- Did I cast the *Yijing* 易经 wrong, Master Obscure?
- Perhaps you asked the wrong question
- I asked: 'what I should do?'
- And not: 'what if I do . . . "This"?'

The Second Time I Went To Chinatown 我去唐人街的第二次

Actually I went to Chinatown lots of times and Ate

And Ate

> NoodlesAndDumplingsAndRiceAndPorkAndFishAnd
> DuckAndHotpotAndNoodlesAndDumplingsAndRice
> AndNoodlesAndDumplingsAndRiceAndNoodlesAnd
> DumplingsAndRiceAnd

But The Second Time I remember there was a protest there in Chinatown

And that got me dreaming I was Chinese again

> – *'Remember. No one cause any trouble or do anything illegal. Let's show people the Chinese can protest without causing trouble or doing anything illegal. And let's be a flagship to other ethnic minorities to show that we can protest without causing trouble or doing anything illegal'*

But then a man in the crowd who doesn't quite look Chinese –

> Someone said he's from Uzbekistan

Starts protesting about China and what China is doing to Uyghurs and Tibetans and Muslims so they bundle the man

> Someone said he's from Uzbekistan

Around the corner where I see punches thrown from the many against the one

> Someone said he's from Uzbekistan

Cloud & Obscure #3 云与晦涩 #三 cont'd again

- A marginal improvement, Middle-aged Cloud

- Praise indeed, Master Obscure

- On superficial viewing it would appear that you're still sighing out nonsense to deceive the crowds but the unreliable narrator technique deployed there leaves the audience constantly guessing and unsettled by the sly race satire of the underlying commentary. Most commendable. Really

- Now I just have to market it

- Market it

- It's no use if it's not heard, Master Obscure. If it's not heard it remains . . . obscure. Master Obscure

- Still you pluck your zither strings to sell your name to the world?

- If no one hears it or connects from it or learns from it or loves it . . . what use is a story?

If you have use

They'll use you up

And they won't remember

They sapped your juice

And filled their cup

After you're dismembered

I'd rather be

A useless tree

Late Stage Capitalist Theatre 晚期资本主义剧院

Virtuosity

Virtuosity

When the Dao is in this world

- That's so cool!

- It was taught me by someone who doesn't want to be named

- So they're . . . obscure?

- They are indeed . . . Obscure

- Were they . . . like . . . your . . . Sage?

- Oh this person doesn't much like / Sages

- 'cuz you talk a lot about Sages in your / story?

- Zhuangzi thought Sages were to blame for all the problems in the world

- Zhuang . . .

- Zhuang / zi

- For those just logging on now and connecting here with Team ESEA Podcast I'm here talking to the celebrated writer, activist and all-round ESEA community leader, The ESEA Butterfly

- Hello

- Tell us about your name, Butterfly? That's not your real name is it?

- I've got a dull English name 'cuz my dad was adopted. I chose Butterfly from Zhuangzi and I chose ESEA because . . . well, that's where I found my identity. As ESEA. I feel I'm very . . . ESEA

– #ESEALove ! And . . . tell us about your book . . . *The Virtuosity of ESEA Community Organising And Self-Care Activism*

– Well. Virtuosity is . . . it's from Zhuangzi / again

– You really know about our ESEA culture don't you!

– Virtuosity is kind of like . . . spiritual charisma

– You say so in your / story

– Yeah, and I figured that, really, that . . . Virtuosity, for me, was all about . . . being seen because . . . too often . . . as ESEAs in the media we've been . . . forced into activism to gain representation in the media /

– That's so true /

– I think it's important for ESEAs to see it's possible for ESEAs to achieve anything through hard work and . . . self-belief and . . . activism

– What do you mean by . . . activism?

– Well, it's . . . I think my presence is . . . as an ESEA . . . my presence proves that . . . it's . . . important to support ESEAs and . . . I do interviews in magazines where I . . . yeah 'cuz . . . representation matters

– Yes you're certainly a . . . RepresentationAsian

– Thank / you

– And you're all dressed up in . . . what is that?

– Oh this, it's a *changshan*

– It's Chinese, right?

– I believe so /

– How do you say it?

– *Changshan*

– *Changshan*

- *Changshan*
- ESEA Culture is so deep /
- Yeah, I'm wearing it because I'm actually on my way to Buckingham Palace after this to meet His Majesty King Charles and Queen Camilla as part of an event celebrating the ESEA community and we're invited to wear national dress, so . . .
- Wow. That's . . . what a win for our community and all your . . . activism
- It certainly feels like the ESEA Community has arrived at last
- Oh and here's our first caller at Team ESEA Podcast, hello, to @WightingTheWong, @WightingTheWong, here you are talking to The ESEA Butterfly themselves
- Hello

When King Wei of Chu wanted to make Zhuangzi a chief minister

Zhuangzi just laughed

And said –

'Have you not seen the victim-ox for the border sacrifice? The clue is in the name. The victim-ox gets lavishly but carefully fed for several years, and draped in gold with rich embroidery so the victim-ox is gaudy enough to enter the Grand Temple . . . where the victim-ox is slaughtered. When the time comes the victim-ox might wish he was just an orphan-piglet'

Changshan *is not Chinese. It's Manchu dress*

Are you going to Chinatown for the protest next week?

'Chinese

'Japanese

'All of these

'In Team ESEA'

The Third Time I Went To Chinatown 我去唐人街的第三次

> *Stop Asian Hate! Stop Asian Hate! Stop Asian Hate!*
>
> *Say hey!*
>
> *Say no!*
>
> *Say Sinophobia has got to go!*

I dreamed I was Chinese again

> *No Cold War! No Cold War!*
>
> *. . . we are here in Chinatown today to send a very clear message about the rise in Sinophobia and racism against Chinese and other East and Southeast Asians / . . .*

The Sage of Chinatown???

> *. . . ever since Covid-19 and we all know why there's this rise in hate against Chinese and other East and Southeast Asians / . . .*
>
> *Stop oppressing Uyghurs!*
>
> *Stop oppressing Hong Kong!*
>
> *Stop oppressing Tibet!*

–   */ because it's all part of the ramping up of US imperialist aggression against China and it's part of a campaign to smear China / because the US imperialist war machine see China as a threat to US imperialist hegemony*

–   *Don't Attack Taiwan! / Geung Feuk Heung Gong, Si Doi Gap Min! Free free the Uyghurs! Free free Tibet! Free free Mongolia!*

> *'. . . these people over there are thugs and terrorists and they have nothing of any sense to say so don't listen to the lies of the Imperialist Western media who just want to lie and smear China and cause instability when what we need is harmony and unity and harmony and unity and harmony and unity and harmony and unity and . . .'*

Sometimes

I dream I'm Chinese –

> Then why do you call us cockroaches and pelt us with eggs when we ask for the right to raise our voices and

> Remember

> Chinese people being crushed by tanks and disappearing and disappearing and disappearing like our History disappears and is

> Replaced by

> Myth

> And Propaganda?

And a fight breaks out under the Chinatown arch and flags are pulled down and all of a sudden

We're not the same any more

> And the heavens open and the rain pours down and

The Sage of Stop Asian Hate roars in the rain like a force of nature that we're all cockroaches and murderers and terrorists and imperial lackeys of the NED funded Western deep-state

> ***'Come down to Chinatown and we'll fight you!'***

I want to dream of being a butterfly

Or be a butterfly dreaming of being me

But I dream

I'm a cockroach

> And because I'm a cockroach and I've raised my Angry Protest Voice I'm chased down a side street by two flag-carrying anti-imperialists

And in that moment I find myself thinking

> Zhuangzi

What would the sage say?

   But Zhuangzi hated sages

He blamed the sages for all the problems of the world

   Maybe that's why I'm so confused

Because of the sages

   And Zhuangzi would probably say something about

Virtuosity

Here

Now

In this back alley off a street they call Chinatown where a mad-eyed dreamer who wants to belong and tell stories and learn to cry is about to be kicked senseless by two angry Chinese men who want to Stop Asian Hate . . .

Ballad of Virtuosity (De 德) 精湛的歌谣

Trouble weighs more than this earth

It's weighed from day of birth

It's a long long long

Way on the wind

It's all wrong wrong wrong

That song you sing

(But who am I to say)

And the days they burn and blaze

And take all that you have made

It's a long long long

Way on the wind

It's all wrong wrong wrong

That song you sing

(But who am I to say)

The Garden of Tonal Harmony 调和花园

-   This place . . .

-   It's safe

-   It's beautiful

-   Smooth

-   That music . . .

-   Soothes and balms /

-   The air. Is this . . .

Is this the Milky Way? The Golden Loom from Heaven? This is surely where the Dao leads. I want to stay Forever. And breathe the air. And taste the fruit on the trees. And write

Our Definitive British Chinese Story

-   It's so good to see you again

-   We've never met

-   But you're . . .

-   You're mistaking me for my sibling Obscure

-   You're not . . . Obscure?

-   I am Opaque. I am Obscure's sibling

-   Opaque. Then where is Obscure?

-   Obscure can't come here

-   Why can't Obscure come here?

-   Master Obscure's Dao is . . . particular

-   I'm confused

-   Of course

-   This place, Master Opaque. It's . . .

- The Garden of Tonal Harmony
- Pangu's Garden of Tonal Harmony?
- Just . . . Garden of Tonal Harmony
- But Pangu /
- We had a change of proprietor
- So beautiful
- Perfect
- It is
- After a long struggle we got here. And now you've joined us
- How . . .
- Did we get here?
- . . .
- Tokens like yourself led us
- We are . . . accepted?
- The tokens are celebrated for their golden exotic glamour
- Their wealth?
- You accomplish nothing without gold
- I was starting to think that
- Our tokens, our /
- Organisors /
- / they made this garden a wonderfully supportive space where we're polite and respectful and kind at all times. And we believe in celebrating the achievements of our community
- Our 'community'

- Our wonderful community
- And this here . . . this . . . lake
- A Lake of Boba Pearls
- Oh my
- Try it
- I can?
- Of course
- . . .
- . . .
- It's
- It really is
- So
- Isn't it?
- It's so sweet
- Sweetness enriches. Sweetness beguiles. Sweetness attains
- It's disgusting
- . . .
- It's the worst fucking boba I've ever tasted. It's . . . garish and sickly. Thick and viscid. And what kind of cassava shrub are those pearls made from? They're like lumps of dung
- It takes time. To acquire the taste
- I'm sorry, I didn't mean to be rude
- That's okay. We encourage honesty here. Respectfully of course
- But, Opaque

– Yes, Cloud

– What is that down there?

– Where?

– At the bottom of the Boba Pearl Lake?

– . . .

– . . .

– . . .

– Is that . . . is that . . . Pangu?

– You know what Pangu looks like?

– Pangu's image comes up on Google

– Pangu is gradually being forgotten

– But Pangu's Story / –

– We're moving on from Pangu

– But Pangu's Story is part of **our** Story

– Pangu Began

– Yes, Pangu Began / everything –

– But it's time for others to Finish what Pangu Began

– Pangu . . . created / –

– Well /

– Didn't Pangu . . . create?

– Pangu's contribution is . . . exaggerated

– But Pangu's voice was said to be like thunder

– We all did our bit /

– Pangu's force was like nature /

– Pangu was aggressive /

– Pangu literally blew the doors open /

– **Pangu is just one creation myth**

– . . .

– Of many

– So how did Pangu get down there? At the bottom of the lake. And clearly dismembered. And clearly . . . Not Living

– . . .

– How???

– Pangu's voice became . . . too much. We had to stop Pangu

– You killed Pangu

– . . .

– You killed Pangu. All of you. Led by the golden tokens the leaders the organisors the . . . keepers of the gate. You killed Pangu and you cut Pangu into pieces and you pushed Pangu into the Boba Lake

– It was . . . a difficult time

– So why leave Pangu down there?

– . . .

– . . .

– You said earlier Pangu . . . created. It's not true of course but Pangu's . . . essence /

– Pangu's sweat and secretions and blood and faeces and semen /

– / contains . . . vitality and /

– De 德

– What is that?

- ...
- You stole Pangu's Virtuosity
- ...
- And you're still stealing it now

Positivity

Positivity

Achievement in the West

The Dao of who's the Best

This sweet and cloying dream

Up there on the screen

Cloud & Obscure #3 and a half because 4 is unlucky in Chinese Culture 云与晦 #三点五因为 四在中国文化中是不吉利的

- Young Cloud

- Master Obscure, it's so good to see you again

- Where have you been, Old Cloud

- I tripped the White fandango, Master Obscure

- You told your story

- I did

- So you're wielding the sun and moon in your hands

- Not quite

- Then?

- I lacked the Virtuosity, Master Obscure

- . . .

- . . .

- Have I ever told you about The Useless Tree?

- That song you sing /

- It begins from the story that Zhuangzi told. The actual Representative Story

- Can I hear it?

There was once a traveller in the state of Qi

The traveller came across an enormous tree

It was over a hundred arm spans round, so big so vast that thousands of oxen could shade under it

It stretched over the surrounding hills, even its lowest branches were hundreds of feet from the ground and at least a dozen of them were big enough they could be hollowed out and made into ships

A local person approached the traveller and said,

'That big tree. It's fucking useless'

The traveller asked why the local person spoke so disparagingly of something so awe-inspiring as this vast and mighty tree

'That tree is worthless and that's how it's gotten to be so big. In the Jingshi region of Song they have huge trees like this as well. The tall ones get chopped down to make monkey perches. The trees that are three or four spans around get chopped down to make pillars for fancy stately homes. If they're seven or eight spans around they get felled to make coffin shells for rich dead people. Trees live a long time but not the useful ones. Useful trees die before their time under axes and saws'

That's the trouble that comes from being worth something

And it's the same with people

If they want your voice they'll cut out your tongue and steal it

If they want to sound like you they'll rip out your whole throat

If they want to see what you see they'll cut out your fucking eyes

If they want to look like you they'll take your whole face and try and wear it

That thing that you think with they'll saw open your skull cut it free and take it

Those things on your hand they'll break them off and use them to point

Those things that you lift with they'll rip them out of your sockets and take them

Those things that you walk on they'll pull and pull till they have them to walk with

That thing that you piss with and fuck with they'll want that as well

They'll even want the thing you shit with because they'll wonder if it shits in a more dynamic way

Those shoulders they stand on they'll want to chisel and hack till they have them to stand on without you there

Even that wrecked front tooth that's distended and mishappen and rotting in your mouth it's your pain and your truth and it's more real than what they've got so they'll want it

That heart that beats inside your chest and carries your flame they'll rip that out of your fucking thorax and try and eat it

But that's just the problem

They can't eat it because it has too much essence and they'll just puke it back up

None of it works because it's still *your* tongue, *your* throat, *your* face, *your* eyes, *your* brain, *your* whole anatomy, *your* shoulders they stood on *your* heart that beat in a time that was fearless and strong

So they're going to have to denigrate you

Devalue you

Dehumanise you

And to do that they're going to have to rewrite your story with the crudest fucking crayon you've ever seen

Because they're clumsy and negligent and solipsistic and selfish

But they'll try and tell the tiny world they occupy how evil you were how cruel you were how vicious you were and to do that they'll have to erase your very being because there's no room for the light and shade and complex patterns of actual living life and their crude fucking crayon is too fucking crude to draw it any way

So your life

That innocent child you were who opened their arms to the world and said 'yes I'm Chinese' and was beaten in the playground for it that child no longer exists because it has no place in their narrative

That father you have who didn't know his own father who was wrenched across the world when he was only a boy and given a white man's name and who worked every menial shift you can even imagine and a few you can't he's no use in their version of the story

That mother you had who got asked if she adopted you when she wheeled you in the pram they won't want to think about her

And that sibling who couldn't make it back from the narcotic dream and left this Dao of heartbreak, tears and racial isolation to be a butterfly in another life, they won't want that actual human tragedy getting in the way of their dank propaganda

Your hopes your dreams your trauma your pain your disappointments your despondence your defiance your daring your determination your dogged insistence your life your loves your losses your laurels they'll bend it and twist and try and toss it into the river but when it floats back up and gives them the finger they'll scribble all over it with their nasty crude crayon and say

You were never here

Because you were effective

Because you made things happen

Because you were useful

All shamans know this

It's better to be useless

With discombobulated virtuosity

And

Dare

To

Dream

Of Being

A Butterfly

–   Thank you, Master Obscure

–   Can you hear her, Master Cloud?

–   I think I can

–   Winding and Twisting

–   She cannot be named

–   Will you Dream, Butterfly?

Positivity Song: Chasing the Butterfly (Dream) 正能量
蝶(梦)

We skipped the White fandango

Granted access by the QUANGO

We rose up from the model token myth

We danced in dazed defiance

Resisted our compliance

We gazed up to the sky in golden bliss

We're flying in the breeze

We're chasing down that dream

Diving out from the boat

To kiss reflections in the stream

We blew the three-act structure

Dramaturgic rupture

   Disruption on the dancefloor with the form

Left our woe there on the wooden O

Our tears there in the iron bowl

   Bent and broke the narrative law

We're flying in the breeze

   We're chasing down that dream

Diving out from the boat

   To our reflection in the stream

Expressionistic wings

   On the throw of the Yijing 易經

Psychedelic tinge

   This butterfly can sing

*You need a zig-zag stride a wig-wag ride a sight-gag slide a ragbag
guide that won't impede your steps in this cosmic mess*

Of your Virtuosity

Keep your feet unharmed

Let it all go!

End.

For a complete listing of
Methuen Drama titles, visit:
www.bloomsbury.com/drama

Follow us on Twitter and keep up to date
with our news and publications
@MethuenDrama